RECRUITMENT: FOR MANAGERS

RECRUITMENT: FOR MANAGERS

R P J Archer

ATHENA PRESS
LONDON

RECRUITMENT: FOR MANAGERS
Copyright © R P J Archer 2009

All Rights Reserved

No part of this book may be reproduced in any form
by photocopying or by any electronic or mechanical means,
including information storage or retrieval systems,
without permission in writing from both the copyright
owner and the publisher of this book.

ISBN 978 1 84748 590 8

First published 2009 by
ATHENA PRESS
Queen's House, 2 Holly Road
Twickenham TW1 4EG
United Kingdom

Printed for Athena Press

Contents

About the Author	7
Introduction	9
Identifying the Need	11
The Sleeper File	15
Specifying the Position and Job Description	17
Sourcing the Candidates	23
The Interview	29
The Induction	41
Summary	45
Recruitment Checklist	46

About the Author

Peter Archer has extensive people-management experience built over many years in both retail and trade businesses, large and small. His first job as a manager was at the age of eighteen, managing a group of men twice his age in a motorcycle dealership. Peter remarked, 'Diplomacy was key'. His last twenty-seven years were spent with EMAP plc, one of the largest publishing and media groups in the UK. His special skill was recruiting the right people and welding them into highly motivated and competitive teams. He was probably one of the best people managers EMAP ever had.

Since his retirement, he has worked as a consultant, using his many years of experience to help companies who face difficult issues in their business. His ability to feel comfortable at all levels, from boardroom to canteen, has helped in finding solutions to what seemed, at the time, insoluble problems. As he often says, 'Problem plus solution equals progress.' His greatest enjoyment is found in turning raw recruits into confident, skilled and competent members of the business.

Introduction

I consider recruitment to be the single most important part of any organisation, and yet it is probably the part that most businesses neglect or get wrong. Having then made this fundamental error, they blame the subsequent problems on everything else. Whenever I hear a manager criticising a member of staff, I always asked the same question: Who recruited them? They may be underperforming for a number of reasons, but often it's because they are either in the wrong job or not qualified for the position they hold. Who is responsible for this error? The recruiter – and that, in turn, usually means the manager. Whether you are recruiting one or a dozen people, the principles of good recruiting are the same and apply to all businesses, large and small.

Too often managers are faced with recruiting staff when they have had little or no training in recruitment. This is a daunting task for any manager and, in these circumstances, guaranteed to result in a failure to recruit effectively. The recruitment process should be an enjoyable time for you, an opportunity to meet new people with great potential and new skills. These new people can be trained to accept more responsibility, thereby freeing up your time to concentrate on ways to move the business forward.

This book is for managers who conduct, or want to

conduct, their own recruitment. However, if the actual recruitment of staff is handled by another department or agency, this book will help you ensure that you get the right people turning up at your door ready to start work. When you have finished reading this book, you might decide to get a lot more involved in deciding who your next member of staff is going to be and how you will deal with their first few days and weeks with the team.

Not many businesses or managers appreciate the hidden cost of recruiting staff. This hidden cost starts when a person begins to switch off because they are leaving. From this moment there is the recruitment process, the new person joining the company and then the time it takes for them to get up to speed. The time this takes and the cost to the company in lost productivity is frightening. The aim of this book is to reduce that time and subsequent cost to a minimum.

I hope this book will help you become a great recruiter and thereby a more effective manager.

Identifying the Need

Some time ago a friend came to me and told me that a woman in his office had asked if he could find room for her sister, who had just lost her job. She said that her sister was hard-working, bright, intelligent, a fun person to be around and would make an admirable addition to the office. I said to him, 'Do you need anyone?'

He said, 'No, not right now, but I didn't want to upset her by saying no.'

I explained that there are some very definite parameters for recruiting staff and helping one of your people find a job for their relative isn't one of them.

All managers face the moment when they say, 'We need to recruit someone.' Well, stop for a moment and consider why you need to recruit. Is it a replacement for someone who is leaving? Short-term cover? Or is it for more staff, which you have fully justified by the stunning plan for expansion or a forthcoming project which you presented to your line manager or director? Or is it because someone is away on maternity leave or off with long-term illness? The reason you want staff will determine your plan of action. Remember, it is vitally important that when taking people on to cover for maternity leave or long-term illness that the person that you take on fully understands that should the person on maternity leave or long-term sick leave wish to return to their old job, the person sitting in their chair will have to give it up. The upside is that while they are with you, they may illustrate skills that you wish to keep, so you may be able to find them another position, either with you or another department, but you must never promise that during the interview.

You should also now take the opportunity to review the requirements and skills for the vacant position and make any changes as necessary. Do not assume that the job has not changed, all jobs change over time.

Do you remember that old saying, 'Too much for one, not enough for two'? This is not a particularly rare situation and is one that most of you will probably have faced a few times. So what is the right way to deal with this? Well, only when the 'one' is on the brink of being overwhelmed should you get that extra person in. If you go for two people too early, you will end up with both of them sitting around twiddling their thumbs. It's Murphy's Law syndrome. The only way you can get Number Two to hit the floor running is, unfortunately, to watch Number One suffer for a bit longer than you, or they, would like. You can always sweeten this with some extra cash as a reward. So, when faced with the 'We need extra staff' situation, make sure you have sufficient work for the extra staff member when they join the team.

I could fill a large hall with the number of people I could have recruited, who would have enriched my life with their wit and humour, but having them in the workplace would have been an utter disaster with people unable to work and hold their sides laughing at the same time. I have also, on occasion, interviewed people who are just awesome in the skills area but put them in a team environment and in no time I would have had a full-scale riot on my hands. These are people who have to work alone and yes, some jobs do require that. The right kind of questions during the interview process will help you to identify who is who.

Maybe you are fully staffed at the moment but remember, as a manager, you are, or should be, constantly talent-spotting. The opportunities to spot new, talented people who you would like to work for you are everywhere, you just have to spot them. They will undoubtedly surface during your normal working day. They may work for a competitor or another department within your company. If they work for another department within your own company, please be professional and observe etiquette – approach their manager first. If faced with an interesting approach from someone expressing an interest in working for you, get them in for an informal chat. Make sure that they understand it is not a formal interview. If you like what you see, tell them if you have a current vacancy or not. If you do, ask them to apply for an interview in the normal way and say you look forward to seeing them again then. If you don't, tell them you will keep in touch and pop their details into the 'sleeper file'.

The Sleeper File

This system can be a truly effective way of speeding up the process of recruiting. Every good manager who handles recruitment should have a sleeper file. In this file are the details of people who you have either met informally to discuss their interest in joining you, or have formally interviewed but were unable to recruit at the time. For example, they could be the close number two in a recent round of interviews. In this case you would explain to the candidate that they were just edged out by another candidate, but you were very impressed by their interview and you would like to remain in touch in case a similar position arises in the near future. I have not interviewed anyone who was not impressed by this interest in them.

Another entry in the sleeper file could be someone who approached you for a job from another department, but you need to explore the political implications before you can process their interest further.

Another entry may follow an interesting approach from a person who asks if you have any vacancies, but you do not at that time.

You may also include people you have approached to see if they were interested in joining your team but, for various good reasons, although keen, they were not able to move jobs at that time.

Bear in mind that there is a sell-by date with this method, so don't be put off if your phone call in three months' time to a sleeper from the file meets with a blank. It may be called a sleeper file, but you need to keep it alive and as up to date as possible.

Once you have identified the need to recruit, you should be ready to organise the interviews within two weeks or sooner. It may not always be possible to sit down with your first interviewee this quickly, but you should make a real effort to do so. Remember, the longer you take, the more it costs the business. A sleeper file will help you to do this. However, if this is not possible, you begin the recruitment process. If you are not personally responsible for recruitment but you want to ensure that you get the right person, then you certainly need to carry out the initial part of this process up to interview stage, followed by the induction procedure. Who knows, after reading this book you may decide to get more involved in the whole process.

Specifying the Position and Job Description

OK, so you have identified a need for one or a number of new or additional staff. Now you start the process of finding the right people. A good practice is to always endeavour to recruit someone better than the person you are replacing, no matter how good they were. This will ensure that you keep standards high.

Irrespective of whether the position is new or not, this is where we start. First you identify or review all the skills needed for the position. Don't rush this part; it is vitally important that you get this absolutely correct to the smallest detail. This is not the job description – that comes later – this is for you to ensure you get the right person with all the necessary skills. Even if this is a straightforward replacement, go over the skills required again, things will have changed. However, to do this effectively you have to understand the skills required for the vacant position inside out. If you are not that familiar with the skills required, get someone who does understand this to help. The other people in the office will appreciate your efforts to get it right and will be happy to help you.

When you have completed that, start work on the competencies. What kind of person do you want? Restate the company and team values. Ideally you want people who hold the same values as you and the rest of the team. Otherwise you are inviting disruption. If it is a position within the team, you need someone who will appreciate team values.

Now hone this down into a formal job description. This will contain:

- the job title
- a description of the job and responsibilities
- who the employee would report to
- the employee's HR contact
- notice period
- key skills
- key purpose (why their job is important and how it interacts with other positions)
- key outcomes of successful execution of the job
- accountabilities
- company and team values

I am constantly amazed by the number of people I come across who do not have a job description. My response to that is, 'So how do you know what your job is?' They seem pretty confident that they do know what their job is, but I wonder how close 'what they think' is to what they should actually be doing. Or even what their manager thinks they should be doing. People are often bawled out for not doing their job when in fact they thought that was exactly what they were doing!

A well-formulated job description is read, understood, agreed and signed to that effect by every new employee. It is there as a constant reference point for both employee and employer. Apart from listing the skill requirements and responsibilities, the job description should also, ideally, have attached the company's work ethic, principles and values.

Together with the technical requirements, you should now have a very good demographic profile of the person or people you are seeking. If you do not recruit personally, now is a good time to talk to the person who will be in charge of the recruitment. Take your job description and list of competencies and tell them that if anyone turns up at your door who does not fit, you will send them straight back.

The following story illustrates how important it is to understand who you are looking for and how the requirements of a job can change. Some years ago I was looking for a production manager to oversee the production of a highly successful national weekly newspaper. As you can imagine, the skill list for this extremely important post was considerable. At that time we were experiencing some awkward problems with the unions at the print works. We were not directly involved, but my production manager had to cross their picket line on a regular basis. So I was going to have to find someone who could also deal with that situation. I had an application from a chap who was a porter at the local hospital. My first thought was he must be applying for a different job. Intrigued, I decided to see him. He told me that he spent most of his time wheeling people in and out of the operating theatre. During the course of our conversation I began to realise that I was talking to a highly intelligent man who was able to deal with some pretty distressing aspects of life in a very capable and humane manner. I also realised that here was a man whom we could train to understand the technical aspects of production but, most importantly, he would be able to deal with our prickly union friends and gain their acceptance. The strike went on for some time, but my new production manager continued to cross their picket line two or three times a day and he always got a cheery greeting from the protesters. The postscript to this story is that he is still there adding value to the company, some twenty-five years later – and of course he now has an extensive knowledge of production.

This is why it is always essential to review the requirements of a job. It also helps to keep an open mind and do not discount less than obvious candidates too quickly.

Sourcing the Candidates

Faced with sourcing your candidates, where do you start? There are a number of sourcing opportunities open to you. The sleeper file, recruitment agencies, paper media, radio, headhunting and the internet.

You will be amazed how much easier your task is now you have a job description and a profile of your prospective candidate.

Be aware that in these days of equal opportunity everyone must be given the opportunity to apply for a vacancy. That applies to your staff, so do not try any quick fixes by moving one of your young, ambitious employees into the vacant position without advertising it within the company for a decent interval first. Many a manager has fallen foul of this one. If one of your people wishes to apply, they should be encouraged to let you know early so that you can either let them down gently or advise them to apply formally and take their chances with all the other candidates. If they complain that it is unfair, just explain that, with their experience of working within the company, they do have an advantage over the other candidates. Remember you are required to fill the vacancy with the best person you can find. If they fail to get the job, then you have some serious work to do on their confidence – and quickly.

Sleeper File

The age of the entries in your sleeper file will determine whether or not you can use this resource. You should always attempt to contact 'sleepers' personally by phone. This gives you the opportunity to check out their reaction first hand. It also allows you to move on quickly should you draw a blank.

Recruitment Agencies

Recruitment agencies can be expensive but they can also be a godsend. It just depends upon your requirements. It is here that your job description will really pay dividends by giving the agency the opportunity to be very accurate in their search. However, do check out their terms of business carefully and make sure that your line manager has agreed to the extra expense.

Paper Media

If you are skilled at putting ads together, then the effect of a well-executed advertisement can be quite stunning. You can actually stop the reader and bring the thought to their mind, 'My God, they're talking to me!' and the effect can be electric. When a recruitment advertisement is well written and reaches out to the person it was specifically written for, it will have that effect. It is not as difficult as it sounds. First, get a really strong picture in your mind of the person you wish to recruit. Think of a headline that will make them stop and look at your ad – not a silly line, but something for them. For example, if your business is in Wimbledon, London and you want local people, then your headline in a London paper could be 'DO YOU LIVE IN WIMBLEDON?' Guess what, everybody who lives in Wimbledon will stop to read your advertisement. I am not suggesting that you use this all the time, but hopefully you get the idea. Now write the ad just to them; imagine you are writing to just that one person. Remember, the object of the exercise is to make the kind of people you want reply to your advertisement and ask for an interview. Keep your copy honest, with no false promises and ignite their interest. If you do not have the necessary copywriting skills then find someone who has and make sure they understand how a good recruitment ad works.

Radio

For effective radio advertising to work it must be repetitive. Personally, I have never used radio for recruitment advertising. However, if I had a business with a high turnover of staff, i.e. seasonal work, part-timers, etc., I would run the ad continuously until it was no longer needed.

Headhunting

If you spot a good prospect, albeit in someone else's company, tread warily. There are professional routes to headhunting, although unfortunately they are not often followed. If it is someone in another department within your own company, please approach their manager first and check if it is OK to talk to them. If it is someone from an outside company, then please conduct your meetings with the utmost discretion. At all times be professional.

The Internet

The internet has now become the preferred method of communication for the majority of people. You should therefore ensure that you make the best use of this resource. Use your own company website if you have one or ask the agencies you are using if and how they intend to use the internet to find prospective candidates.

★

Remember that all your efforts to communicate to prospective candidates, apart from when you use agencies, are geared to encourage them to want to talk to you and learn more about the position.

The Interview

Having gone to some considerable effort to get this far and pull together a stunning group of prospective candidates, do not blow it now. It is at this stage that the worst mistakes are made and the company carries the can. However, this is not going to happen to you.

Responses

Having sifted through all the replies to your advertisement or from the agency, you have to decide whom you want to see. You should aim for a reasonable number of people to meet, simply because it improves your chances of finding the right person. You also have to decide on the time frame you are giving yourself to find a suitable candidate. Do you only have one day or can the interviews be completed in two? Only you can answer this.

Not all responses come as you would expect them. I once had a response to an ad we ran for an ad designer. This chap sent me a six-pack. Six bottles containing real beer. However, he had very cleverly altered the packaging of the carton and the labels on the bottles to contain his CV and all relevant personal details. He felt this unique approach would get him an interview. Of course, I had to see him. Unfortunately, he didn't get the job. It was a speed thing – he could not work to a deadline – but I just knew he was going to end up famous somewhere, I hope he did.

Now, please do this for me. Please reply to those people who do not make it to the interview. I cannot believe the number of people who apply for interviews and never hear another thing. It is simply not professional.

Write to your fortunate list of hopefuls giving them clear instructions as to the date and time of the interview and how to find you. Also ask them to let you know if there is a problem with the date or time. If their application is good enough, you may wish to reschedule an interview if they cannot make the time you suggest.

Conducting the Interview

Conducting an interview correctly is hard work. The level of concentration required in order to maintain the same degree of effort for every interview is energy sapping. So, when you plan the day, make sure you can handle it. Ripping through eight sessions in eight hours is no good for anyone, least of all for the poor people you are interviewing. There is no standard time for how long an interview should take (although an hour is about right) or how many you need before you make a decision. It all depends upon the job, the candidates, what you need to learn from them and how much you need to cover during the course of your search.

Although hard work, interviewing can be a very enjoyable exercise. You are going to meet some very interesting people, people who you could spend some years working alongside. There is great talent out there and you could be in the process of bringing some of that into the company. However, if you have trouble meeting people for the first time and falling easily into conversation, then you have a problem. It is at this point that you must decide to run the interview two-up. By that, I mean that the interview will be conducted by someone else and you sit in purely as an observer. Do you have to be there at all? Yes, because you would be the candidate's manager and you are going to make the final decision on whether to offer them the job or not. Two opinions are better than one. If you do decide to have someone sit in with you, make sure they understand why they are there and what part they play in the questioning. Make them part of your planning process.

Spend some time thinking about how you are going to conduct these interviews. If you decide the interview is going to last an hour, then plan that hour, preferably in the days before you meet them. Use an A4 page and note down the candidate's relevant facts, plus any important questions that may have arisen out of their application.

Write a list of times down the side of your page. Against each time write where you should be in the interview. You will be surprised how you can lose track of the time as the interviews progress.

Spend some time thinking about where you are going to conduct these interviews. Are you using one of your own meeting rooms, or are you going outside to a hotel? Which venue would suit your purpose best?

How will you set out the room? Are you going sit either side of a desk? Make sure they know which is their chair. It would be rather awkward if, after carefully planning your layout, they plonk themselves down in the strategically placed chair you had lined up for yourself. Don't sit higher than them in an effort to intimidate them. Don't sit with your back to a bright window – after twenty minutes you will appear as a black blob. Put your watch on the table where you can see it – there is nothing worse than pulling your sleeve back to see what the time is during an interview.

The whole idea is to get the best out of the interviewee and you will not do that by frightening the life out of them or making it so tough that they cannot demonstrate their true potential. I have come across some amazing horror stories where people have set out to scare the living daylights out of someone just to see how they would react. Just remember, you are not recruiting for the SAS.

The Interview

For me, the first ten seconds is really important: how they enter the room, the look on their face, the grasp of your hand, if they are dressed smartly, the polite wait for you to start. You learn an awful lot about people in those first few seconds. Having invited them into your pre-planned area, allow them a chance to get their breath back by giving them a short résumé of your company and your role in it. Two minutes of small talk relaxes people wonderfully. Then you can settle into the interview.

In the space of an hour – any more and you start to lose the pace – you have got to find out as much as you can about this person. Of course, you have their CV, but this doesn't tell you much about the individual. When I write to people advising them of their place on the list of interviewees, I usually ask them to send me a short letter about themselves in their own handwriting. You'd be amazed how badly some people write and how appalling their spelling is. I know word processors rule our lives, but we should still be able to string two sentences together in our own hand. Try to adopt the 20/80 rule. This is where you speak 20% of the time and listen to them for the other 80% of the time. However, don't let them dominate the conversation. At one interview I couldn't get a word in edgeways. When I had had enough of this, I put my hand up and said, 'Stop! Sorry, but I do have to ask you one or two questions myself!'

During the interview you should go through a series of pre-planned questions that you need answers to. These are questions that have arisen from the candidate's CV or attached handwritten letter. You will also be probing their professed knowledge of the skills you require. You need to tease out their likes and dislikes. It is during these questions that you should learn whether they are a team player or not. While all this is going on, and this is may be where you find that having someone else with you may help, you should observe the candidate as a person. Do you warm to them? Are you enjoying their personality? How do you think the team will take to them? Do you like them? We spend most of our lives at work and it makes that time, which can often be stressful, more enjoyable if we are working with people we like.

Here are some general interview questions which you may find useful. You can weave them into your questions relating to the skills of the job.

1. How did you manage to get time off to come to this interview?
2. Why do you want to leave your current job?
3. What are the things at work which annoy you the most?
4. What is the best and worst experience you have had at work?
5. What would your commuting time to this office be and how would you travel?
6. What interests you about this position?
7. Tell me about the best and worst bits of working in a team.
8. How do you react to criticism?
9. What will you do if you do not get this job?

As you can see, these questions are all about finding out how people think rather than whether they are qualified for the job. One question I really abhor is, 'Where do you want to be in five years' time?' I really cannot see the point of it, especially as the person who asks it has, invariably, no more of a clue to the answer than the person they ask.

Never discount someone because they live a long way from the place of work. They are obviously aware of that and so have a good reason for applying. If they fit your criteria, then get them in. For example, they may be moving into the area next week. However, if they live a long way from the place of work and do not intend to move, ask them how they intend to deal with that. Initial enthusiasm always shortens the distance to travel, but not for long.

Here's a tip: if you are looking for a phone operator, get them to phone in and carry out your initial interview by phone. Remember, you are employing a voice and a telephone manner; how they look is irrelevant.

Make sure that you are honest and tell your interviewees exactly what the job entails – the upsides and the downsides. For example, 'It's really hard work here, but we have fun and enjoy doing it.'

Common sense and honesty play a big part during the course of an interview, but if you are unfortunate enough to come up against a dishonest trickster, don't worry – it will surface very quickly once they start work and you can remedy the error immediately. Everyone should be given a three-month probationary period at the start of their employment, with a week's notice by either side. This allows both the employee and employer to rectify any mistakes quickly. What should you do if this happens and your new employee leaves? Quickly go to the second-choice candidate from the interviews, now sitting in your sleeper file. If you parted on good terms with the second-choice candidate you will usually find that they are more than happy to take up your late offer.

If you decide you need to get people back for a second interview, make sure you give them something to do – like a short presentation for instance. Whatever you decide, you must stretch them on this second visit. Also remember that second interviews require just as much planning as the first.

If you are interviewing a number of people, be aware how difficult it is to remember their faces. I always use a ten-minute period between interviews to put down my thoughts on the interview and a short physical description so I can remember the candidate more easily. You could, of course, use a digital camera. Make sure you ask the candidate's permission first, though. I also score them out of five. 1–2 is a no. 3–4 is a possible. 5 is a definite or second interview. If you end up with three or four 5s then you have the difficult task of selecting a winner and talking the others into remaining keen for another possible opportunity. However, if they are all 1–2s and you are struggling to find the right person, whatever you do don't choose someone out of desperation. It is far better to suffer being short of staff than to employ a third-rate choice. Believe me, I've been there and it's not worth it!

It sometimes happens that, during the course of an interview, you will begin to realise that the person sitting in front of you is applying for a job for which they are just not suited. However, at the same time they illustrate perfectly the skills you need for another position.

I was interviewing a young man for the position of sales representative. It soon became plain to me that he was never going to make a salesman. It just so happened that at the same time we were in the process of setting up a new department which was primarily administrative. This chap was the perfect person to run that department. I shall never forget the look on his face when I said, 'Look, I don't really think this particular job is for you; however, I have something else which I think may be of interest to you. Would you like me to explain it to you?' When I finished explaining he said, 'Yes, please, that's for me.' Try to remain open-minded during the interview process; you never know what may turn up.

OK, so all the interviews have finished, you have studied your notes (usually quietly at home) and you have made your choice. Now it's time for the reaction test. During the course of the interview, I always ask for a phone number where the candidate can be contacted during the day. I promise complete confidentiality; I will do this even to the point of saying I am a friend or relative. I use the daytime to make this call because if it goes wrong I need time to recover the situation quickly. So, you call them on the phone and the conversation goes something like this: 'Hi, Bill, this is Peter Archer, how are you? That's good. Well, Bill, I have had a chance to review all the applications now and have decided that I would very much like to offer the position of Techno Chief to you.'

What they say next is of vital importance. What I want to hear is relief, excitement and a really enthusiastic acceptance of the position. If they say (and this has happened, I think, once) 'Well, thank you, Peter, but do you mind if I think about it?' I then reply, 'Well, I am sorry, Bill, but I have just thought about it too and I am sorry to tell you that I have changed my mind.' I then go to my second choice or start again.

Harsh, you might say, but look at it this way, when someone comes to work for you, they have got to come with a genuine enthusiasm and excitement for that job. If, after due consideration, they are still unsure or it is just to fill the hours between nine and five-thirty, then they are never going to contribute fully to the team's efforts. And that goes for everyone, right down to the cleaning lady – her role is just as important to the smooth running of the office as everyone else's are. I have often said that I would like, just once, someone to reach over, grab me by the lapels and say, 'Look, I really do want this job.' It has never happened, but I have interviewed people where it came close, they were that keen.

References

References are vitally important. You need at least two; three would be better. The references should be on the CV; if not, make sure you get them before they leave the interview. As soon as you have made your verbal offer and it is accepted, follow this up with your formal letter offering the position (subject to references). A copy is then duly signed as acceptance of your offer by your new employee and returned. Then write to – or, better still, phone – the people who have been nominated for references and ask them for a brief view of the successful applicant. Until you receive at least two acceptable references, you cannot fully complete the process of employing your new person.

The Induction

Induction is the period of time between the new person joining the company and them becoming a productive member of the team. How you manage this period will determine whether you get the best or worst from your decision to employ them. Even if you are up to your eyes in work, stop and take the time to do this properly. The moment the new person shows up for work is an important moment in both their lives and the lives of those they will be working with. Prepare them and the people they will be joining well and you will reap the rewards. You will never regret the time taken. The position they are going to occupy will dictate what you need to do. Ideally, whatever the position, the newcomer needs sufficient information about the company and team they are about to join as soon as possible. The team, in turn, need to know about their new colleague. Don't build them up too much, let the team make their own judgements on their abilities.

Although the initial introductions and tour of the office need to be carried out by you, it would be quite in order if you wish to then put your trembling new person into the hands of another – making sure, of course, that the person given this responsibility fully understands what is required and how important their role in the induction process is. If you do this, it does not mean you can now forget about the new person. The responsibility of ensuring the induction process runs smoothly and is successful rests squarely upon your shoulders. Never confuse the word 'delegation' with 'abdication'.

It is also at this time that you should sit down with your new employee and go through the job description. It is vitally important that they both understand and agree with all of it and they must sign to that effect. You should now have their signed agreement to both their letter of appointment (which details their start date, salary and notice period) and their job description. Believe me, this will save you a lot of problems in the future if things do not work out as planned.

I was once faced with employing three senior managers at the same time. We had rearranged the sales departments and I now had three brand-new sales departments fully staffed, just waiting for their managers to turn up. I was extremely lucky in that I managed to find three really good managers in my first attempt. I guess I must have followed my own advice. The hard part now was introducing them to three very streetwise groups of people. The temptation was to get them in quickly as I was getting 'When are we going to see our managers?' on a daily basis. I knew I had to get it right so, for a whole week in a room in a nearby hotel, I kept my managers out of sight. Every day we went through the basics of the operation. Managers came from other departments and presented to them on how their own departments worked and how they interacted with the departments of the new managers.

At the end of that week, they had all the information they needed to slip seamlessly into their new roles. I then introduced them to their new teams. I knew I had got it right when people kept coming up to me wanting to know how these new managers knew so much.

Induction is very much a part of the recruitment process and does not officially end until the new employee has successfully completed their three-month probationary period and is welcomed as a permanent member of staff. However, subject to their performance, you may be able to slip seamlessly from induction to coaching before their three-month probationary period has ended.

"HI, I'M THE NEW MEMBER OF THE TEAM"

Summary

If you remember, I started this book by referring to managers who complain about the inefficiencies of their staff instead of questioning the recruitment process.

It is always harder and takes much longer to do a job well. In the busy business world of today, it requires an iron will to say, 'I will take the time to do this properly.' The benefits of recruiting well are too high to ignore. By recruiting quickly you will save thousands of pounds of lost productivity. By recruiting well you will ensure that the business continues to move forward and the quality of your staff continues to grow.

Happy recruiting.

Recruitment Checklist

- ☐ Do I really need more staff?
- ☐ Is this a permanent or temporary position?
- ☐ Has the job changed? If so, how?
- ☐ Re-evaluate the skills required.
- ☐ Write the job description.
- ☐ Decide upon the method you will use to source the candidates.
- ☐ Select the candidates for the interview.
- ☐ Decide upon an appropriate venue for the interviews.
- ☐ Decide if you will have someone with you.
- ☐ Plan the layout of the room.
- ☐ Plan the interview.
- ☐ Go through the results of the interviews carefully. Make a decision.
- ☐ Contact your first choice by phone.
- ☐ Write your formal letter of appointment.
- ☐ Get signed agreement of the letter of appointment.
- ☐ Obtain the references.
- ☐ Plan the induction process.

- ☐ Brief the new person.
- ☐ Explain the job description and get an agreement and signature.
- ☐ Brief the team.
- ☐ Enjoy the benefits of a job well done.

www.ingramcontent.com/pod-product-compliance
Lightning Source LLC
Chambersburg PA
CBHW031553210526
45464CB00003B/1290

*9 7 8 1 8 4 7 4 8 5 9 0 8 *